A Family House

by Ethan Cruz
illustrated by Renate Lohmann

Core Decodable 109

Mc Graw Hill Education

Bothell, WA • Chicago, IL • Columbus, OH • New York, NY

MHEonline.com

Send all inquiries to:
McGraw-Hill Education
8787 Orion Place
Columbus, OH 43240

ISBN: 978-0-02-145828-8
MHID: 0-02-145828-6

Printed in the United States of America.

7 8 9 LCR 25 24 23

Dean, Mom, and the baby sat on a grassy hill.
A tractor dug below. The tractor dug a deep hole.

The tractor piled dirt on the field's edge.

"That hole will be the basement," explained Mom. "And trucks will haul that dirt away."

Dean was happy. This hole was the start of a new house. It was his family's new house! He felt lucky.

A week later, Dean and Mom came back. The hole now had cement walls. On top, it had four steel beams.

"Steel beams will hold up the house," said Mom.

Three weeks later, Dean was back. A team of four carpenters hammered.

The frame went up quickly. Dad also came to check the house.

Dad pointed. "You will sleep in a bedroom there."

Dean liked seeing the team. He learned a lot.

Dean took a deep breath. He liked smelling fresh wood.

Several teams were in the house. Men put in pipes. Some pipes were for water. Some were for gas. Gas will heat the house.

Electric wires were added. Wires were put in walls.

It takes a lot of know-how to get the wires right.

A crew laid bricks. The bricks were red. The crew put each brick in by hand. It took skill and time.

Weeks passed. Walls were plastered. Lights and switches were added. Painters came. Soon the house was almost ready.

Four trees were planted. Carpenters put a deck on the back of the house.

"We will eat there at times," said Mom.

Finally, after weeks and weeks, the house was ready. A big van brought beds, dressers, desks, and tables.

The family of four stood on the grassy hill. They looked at the new house below.

"We are so lucky," Dean said.